GARFIELD

Classics

Volume Eighteen

MY EIGHTEENTH CLASSIC COLLECTION
CONTAINS:

I AM WHAT I AM!

KOWABUNGA!

DON'T ASK!

JiM DAViS

First published by Ravette Publishing 2006.
Reprinted 2008

Printed and bound in Great Britain
for Ravette Publishing Limited,
Unit 3, Tristar Centre,
Star Road, Partridge Green,
West Sussex RH13 8RA

ISBN: 978-1-84161-251-5

GARFIELD

I Am What I Am!

JiM DAViS

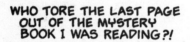

BOY, IT'S BORING IN HERE!

I COULDN'T HAVE DONE IT WITHOUT YOU, ODIE

JIM DAVIS 9-4

WE ALL HAVE TO LIVE TOGETHER

WE HAVE TO BE CONSIDERATE OF OUR NEIGHBORS

SO RETURN THOSE TO MRS. FEENY!

CAN I KEEP THE PEARLS?

JIM DAVIS 9-11

WHOOOOMP!

BUNGEE DOGGGG!

SCRIBBLE SCRIBBLE
SCRIBBLE

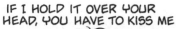

GARFIELD

Kowabunga!

JIM DAVIS

www.garfield.com

Distributed by Universal Press Syndicate

JIM DAVIS 3-18

GARFIELD

Don't Ask!

JIM DAVIS

NEW HAT?

THANKS FOR NOTICING

JiM DAViS 6-8

WE CANCEL EACH OTHER OUT

JIM DAVIS 6·22

JIM DAVIS 7-24

www.garfield.com

JIM DAVIS 7-29

www.garfield.com

Distributed by Universal Press Syndicate

OTHER GARFIELD BOOKS AVAILABLE

Pocket Books		Price	ISBN
Am I Bothered?		£3.99	978-1-84161-286-7
Below Par		£3.50	978-1-84161-152-5
Compute This!		£3.50	978-1-84161-194-5
Don't Ask!		£3.99	978-1-84161-247-8
Feed Me!		£3.99	978-1-84161-242-3
Get Serious		£3.99	978-1-84161-265-2
Gotcha!		£3.50	978-1-84161-226-3
I Am What I Am!		£3.99	978-1-84161-243-0
I Don't Do Perky		£3.99	978-1-84161-195-2
Kowabunga		£3.99	978-1-84161-246-1
Numero Uno	(new)	£3.99	978-1-84161-297-3
Pop Star		£3.50	978-1-84161-151-8
S.W.A.L.K.		£3.50	978-1-84161-225-6
Time to Delegate	(new)	£3.99	978-1-84161-296-6
Wan2tlk?		£3.99	978-1-84161-264-5
What's Not to Like?		£3.99	978-1-84161-285-0

Theme Books	Price	ISBN
Creatures Great & Small	£3.99	978-1-85304-998-9
Entertains You	£4.50	978-1-84161-221-8
Healthy Living	£3.99	978-1-85304-972-9
Pigging Out	£4.50	978-1-85304-893-7
Slam Dunk!	£4.50	978-1-84161-222-5
Successful Living	£3.99	978-1-85304-973-6
The Seasons	£3.99	978-1-85304-999-6

2-in-1 Theme Books	Price	ISBN
All In Good Taste	£6.99	978-1-84161-209 6
Easy Does It	£6.99	978-1-84161-191 4
Lazy Daze	£6.99	978-1-84161-208 9
Licensed to Thrill	£6.99	978-1-84161-192 1
Out For The Couch	£6.99	978-1-84161-144 0
The Gruesome Twosome	£6.99	978-1-84161-143 3

Classics	Price	ISBN
Volume One	£6.99	978-1-85304-970-5
Volume Two	£6.99	978-1-85304-971-2
Volume Three	£6.99	978-1-85304-996-5
Volume Four	£6.99	978-1-85304-997-2
Volume Five	£6.99	978-1-84161-022-1
Volume Six	£6.99	978-1-84161-023-8
Volume Seven	£5.99	978-1-84161-088-7
Volume Eight	£5.99	978-1-84161-089-4
Volume Nine	£6.99	978-1-84161-149-5
Volume Ten	£6.99	978-1-84161-150-1
Volume Eleven	£6.99	978-1-84161-175-4
Volume Twelve	£6.99	978-1-84161-176-1
Volume Thirteen	£6.99	978-1-84161-206-5

Classics (cont'd ...)	Price	ISBN
Volume Fourteen	£6.99	978-1-84161-207-2
Volume Fifteen	£5.99	978-1-84161-232-4
Volume Sixteen	£5.99	978-1-84161-233-1
Volume Seventeen	£6.99	978-1-84161-250-8
new titles available June 2008 ...		
Volume Nineteen	£6.99	978-1-84161-303-1
Volume Twenty	£6.99	978-1-84161 304-8

Gift Books (new series)		
Don't Know, Don't Care	£4.99	978-1-84161-279-9
Get a Grip	£4.99	978-1-84161-282-9
I Don't Do Ordinary	£4.99	978-1-84161-281-2
Keep your Attitude, I have my own	£4.99	978-1-84161-278-2
30 Years - The Fun's Just Begun (new)	£9.99	978-1-84161-307-9

Little Books		
C-c-c-caffeine	£2.50	978-1-84161-183-9
Food 'n' Fitness	£2.50	978-1-84161-145-7
Laughs	£2.50	978-1-84161-146-4
Love 'n' Stuff	£2.50	978-1-84161-147-1
Surf 'n' Sun	£2.50	978-1-84161-186-0
The Office	£2.50	978-1-84161-184-6
Zzzzzz	£2.50	978-1-84161-185-3

Miscellaneous		
Colour Collection Book 2 (new)	£10.99	978-1-84161-306-2
Colour Collection Book 1	£10.99	978-1-84161-293-5
Treasury 7	£10.99	978-1-84161-248-5
Treasury 6	£10.99	978-1-84161-229-4
Treasury 5	£10.99	978-1-84161-198-3
Treasury 4	£10.99	978-1-84161-180-8
Treasury 3	£9.99	978-1-84161-142-6

All Garfield books are available at your local bookshop or from the publisher at the address below.

Just send your order with your payment and name and address details to:-

Ravette Publishing, Unit 3, Tristar Centre, Star Road, Partridge Green, West Sussex RH13 8RA
(tel: 01403 711443 ... email: ravettepub@aol.com)

Prices and availability are subject to change without notice.

Please enclose a cheque or postal order made payable to **Ravette Publishing** to the value of the cover price of the book/s and allow the following for UK postage and packing:-

70p for the first book + 40p for each additional book
except Treasuries & Colour Collections... when please add £3.00 per copy